I0391005

Little Bitty

Book of

Haiku

Veronica Valles

Everyday Sacred

Dallas, Texas

2013

Printed in the United States

First Edition

ISBN: 978-1-304-68432-5

Design and photographs by

Veronica Valles

www.lulu.com

To all who

Haiku.

Keep your eyes open,

Your heart smiling

&

Keep writing!

haiku   **hai·ku** (Noun)

A Japanese poem of seventeen syllables, in three lines of 5/7/5, traditionally evoking images of the natural world.

Haiku is simple, focusing on nature and is about direct experience and expression.

I don't know when I found Haiku. Or, rather, Haiku found me. All I know once we fell in love it was an amazing affair seeing life fully and laying down those moments in simple verse.

Why Haiku?

It's simple.

It's fun.

It keeps me present.

It keeps me engaged with words.

It opens my eyes and heart to the world.

Here's the game –

Throughout these pages are original photos
for you to play with.

Write two Haiku for the same photo.

More if it calls you.

There will be blank pages for you to do so.

At the end of the book you will have plenty of
room to fill the pages with your own daily
observations. Go out and SEE the World.
Experience it. Listen. Drink it in. Taste
colors. Bring it to the page.

Are you ready?

Let's GO!

Remember:

5

7

5

Open your heart

Let it flow

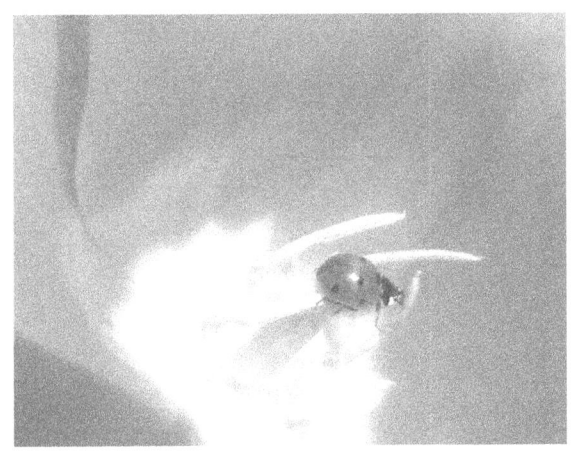

Ladybug Lounge

Beauty out on the edge

Tulip territory dance

Getting ready to fly.

Ladybug Lounge

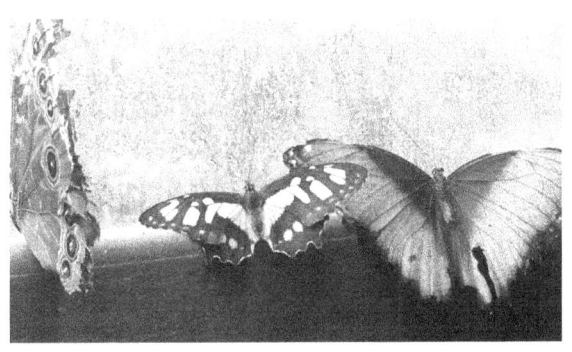

Tres Amigos – La Paz Waterfalls,

Costa Rica

Wondering where to fly

Wishing we were free to be

In the waterfalls.

Tres Amigos – La Paz Waterfalls,

Costa Rica

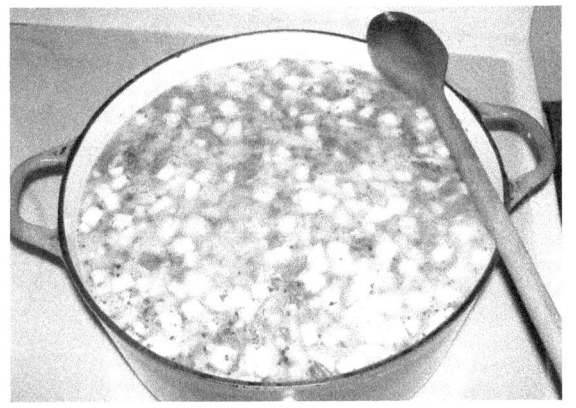

Mamma's Minestrone

On the kitchen stove

Scrumptious love is cooking now

Happy Belly Dance

Mamma's Minestrone

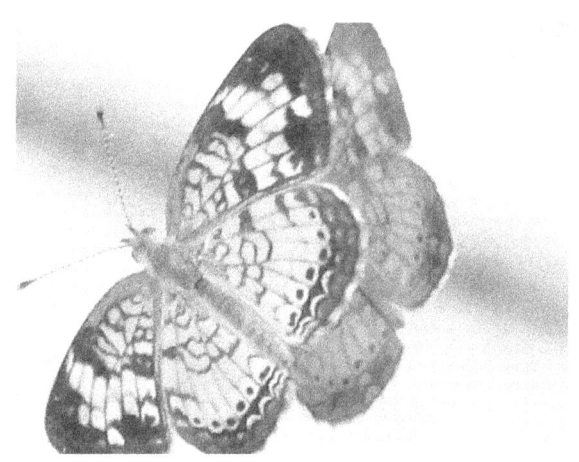

Mirror, Mirror

Looking at myself

I see only GOD smiling

Winking back at me

Mirror, Mirror

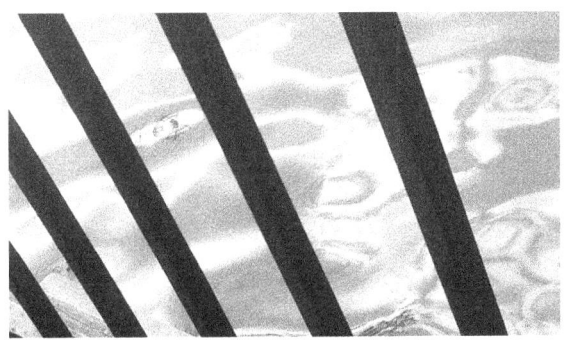

Wavy Blue – Austin, TX

Wavy, gravy blue

Clouds swirling upon the lake

The sky brought to Earth

Wavy Blue – Austin, TX

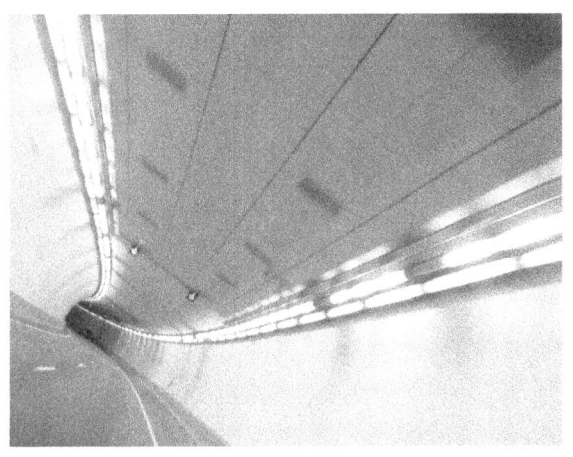

Curved Uncertainty

Into the unknown

Moving at a rapid speed

Life's uncertainty

Curved Uncertainty

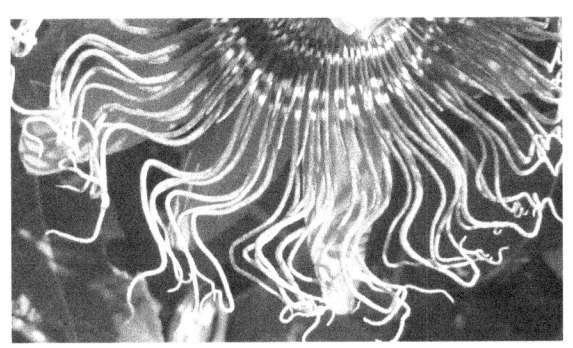

Purple Rays

Your swirling color

Makes me want to dance with you

Into the sunshine

Purple Rays

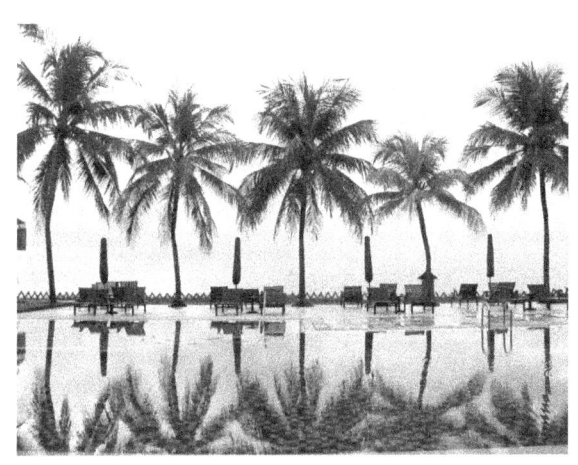

Relaxation –Bali

In palm tree heaven

I can feel peace deep within

Balinese Beauty.

Relaxation -Bali

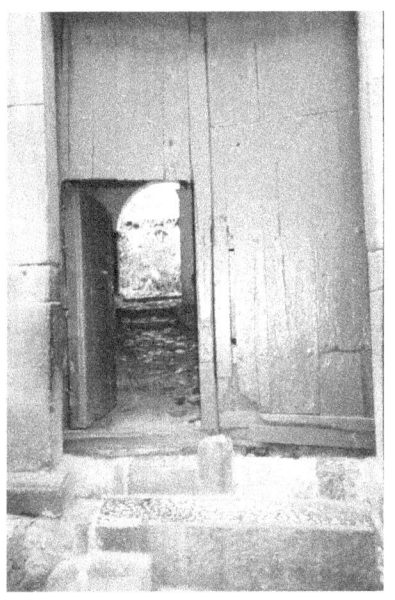

Blue Door - Cusco, Peru

Behind the closed door

Paradise waiting for me

An ancient portal.

Blue Door - Cusco, Peru

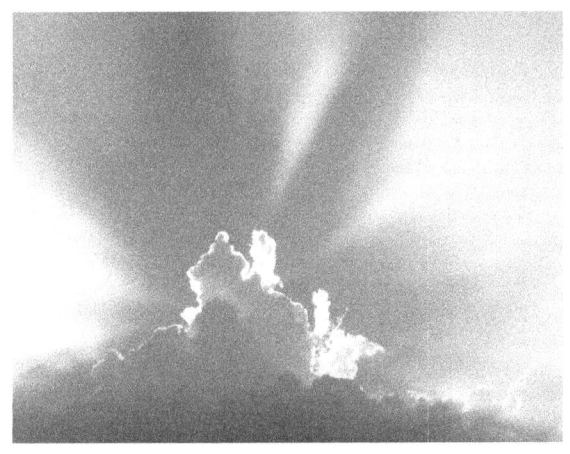

Amazing Grace

Sunrays sculpt the sky

I stand here receiving it

Amazing Grace kiss.

Amazing Grace

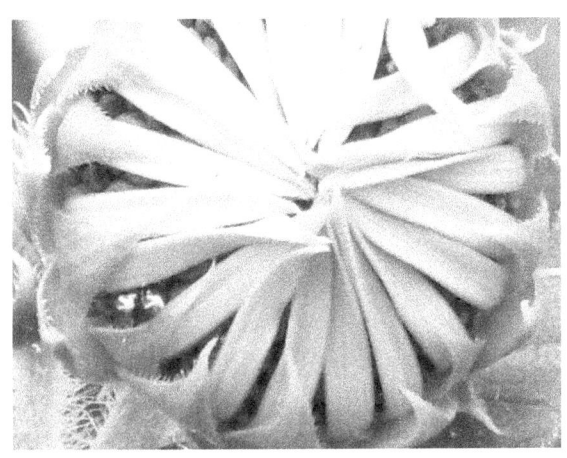

Opening Beauty

When you are ready

To open to your Beauty

You will feel freedom

Opening Beauty

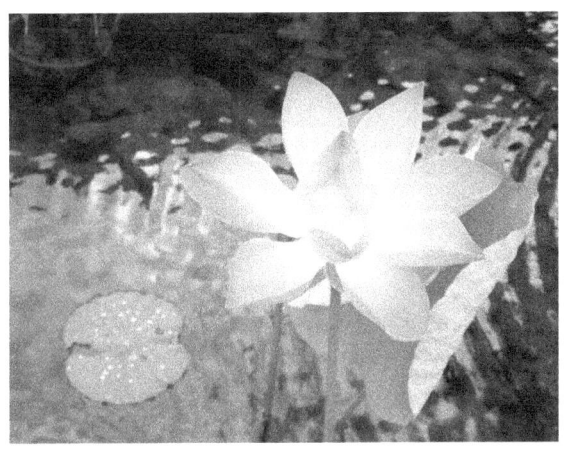

Pink Lotus – Bali

In the mud you rise

A beautiful reminder

Persistence of Peace

Pink Lotus – Bali

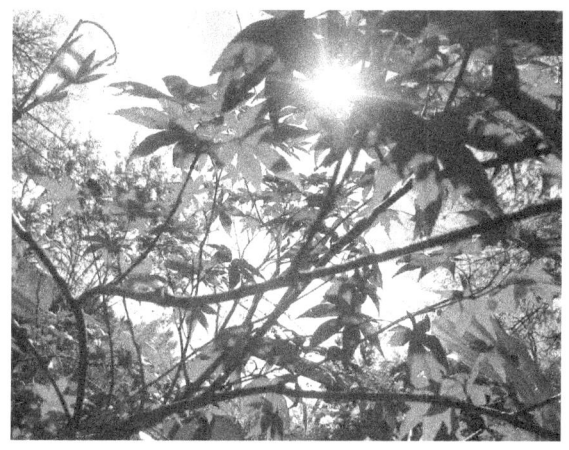

Fire Beauty

A fire fall beauty

I drink the wine of good-bye

Until another bloom

Fire Beauty

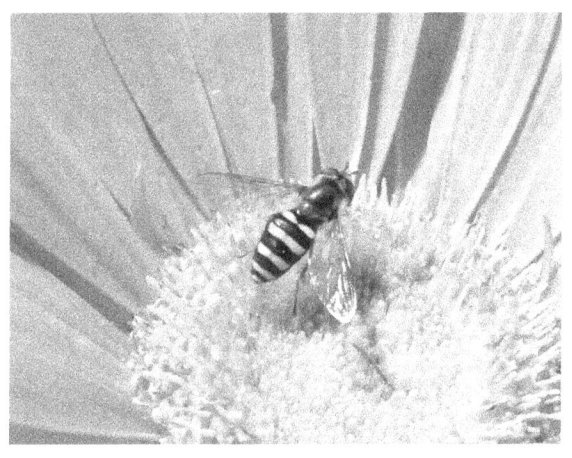

Oh, honey....

Busy bee in motion

Gathering of the pollen

Oh, golden honey…

Oh, honey….

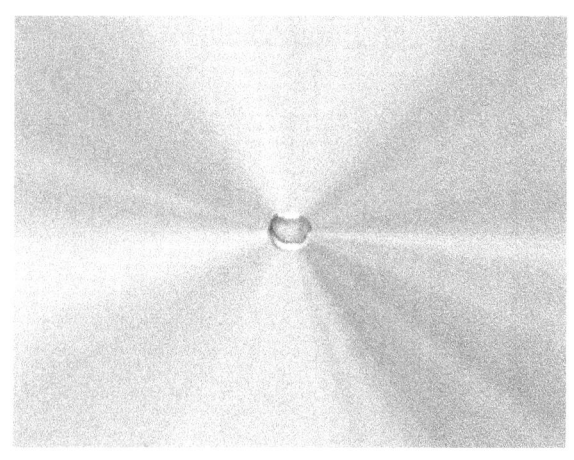

Shout Out!

Every time I speak

I shout out my love for all

Radiating pink.

Shout Out!

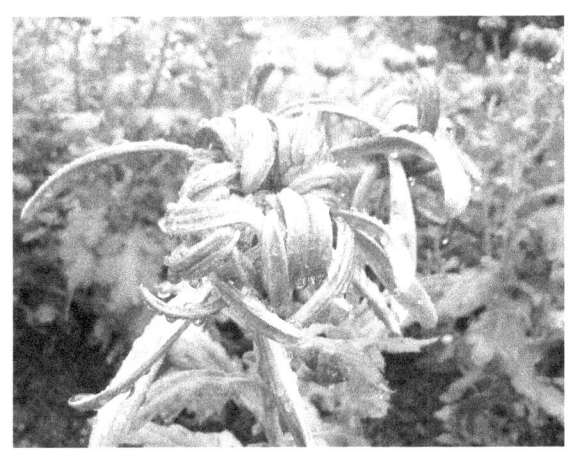

Crazy Love

This crazy love is

Drenching me in fall droplets

I can't shake it off.

Crazy Love

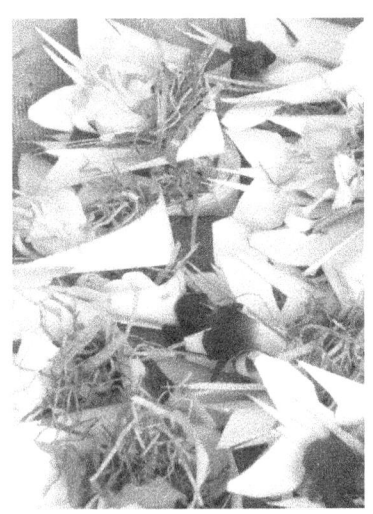

Floral Prayers

Purple, fuschia, red

Prayer offerings to God

Beauty in the word.

Floral Prayers

What do YOU see?

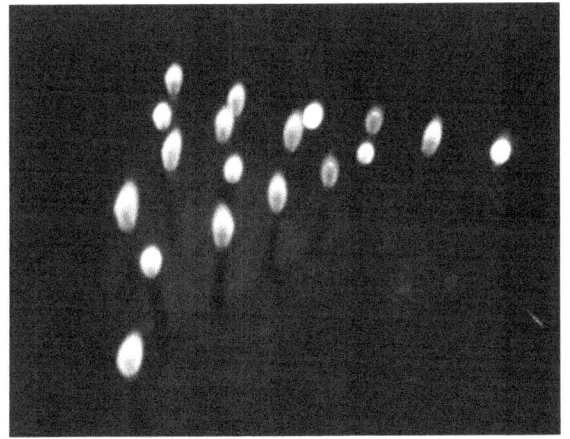

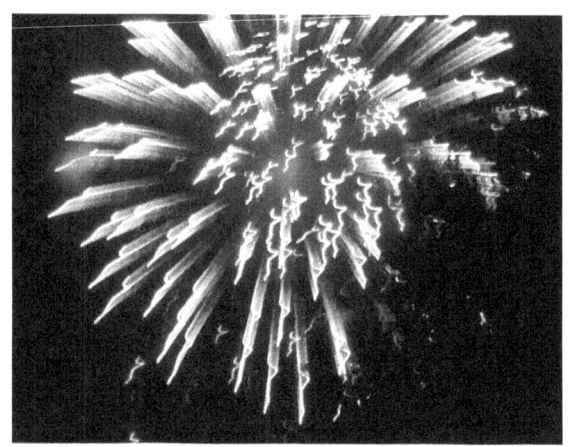

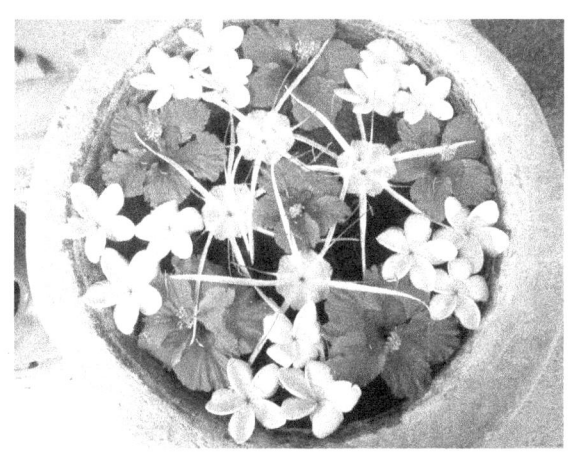

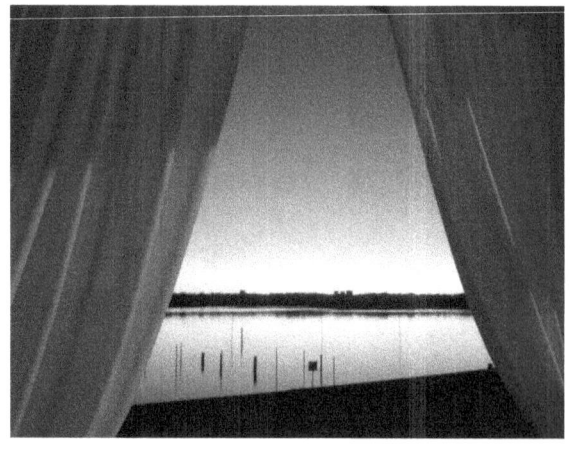

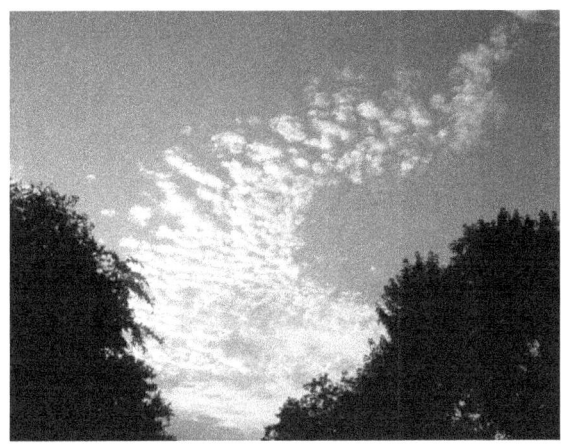

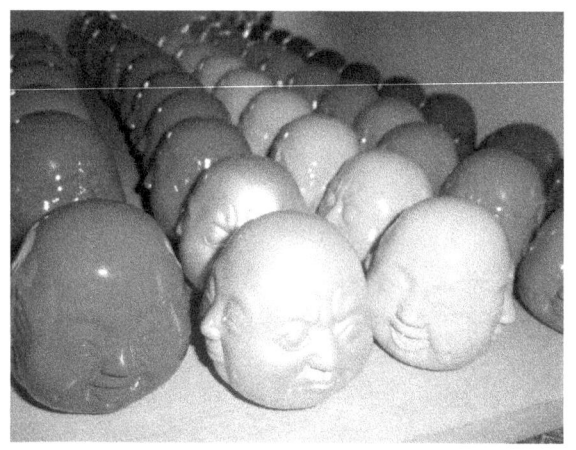

HAVE FUN

Daily…write 5 Haikus

Put them together in a book

Share them with the world

Inspire others.

May you always be

Awake

Aware

Alive

To the Beauty

All around you.

Haiku to YOU.

Always.

~ Veronica Valles

December 4, 2013

www.ingramcontent.com/pod-product-compliance
Lightning Source LLC
Chambersburg PA
CBHW072243170526
45158CB00002BA/992